MAKING THE GRADE · GRADE 1

EASY POPULAR PIECES FOR YOUNG PIANISTS. SELECTED AND ARRANGED BY LYNDA FRITH

Exclusive Distributors:
Hal Leonard Europe Limited
42 Wigmore Street
Marylebone, London, W1U 2RN
Email: info@halleonardeurope.com

This book © Copyright 1991 Chester Music
ISBN 978-0-7119-2526-7
Order No. CH59253
Cover designed by Pemberton & Whitefoord.
Typeset by Capital Setters Limited.

Printed in the EU

Chester Music

INTRODUCTION

This collection of 19 popular tunes has been carefully arranged and graded to provide attractive teaching repertoire for young pianists. New concepts and techniques are introduced progressively, and the familiarity of the material will stimulate pupils' enthusiasm and encourage their practice. The standard of the pieces progresses to Associated Board Grade 1.

CONTENTS

HOWARDS' WAY

by Leslie Osborne & Simon May

This is the theme tune from the popular television series about yachts and sailing.
Let the music flow freely. Notice the stretch between the right hand thumb
and first finger in bars one and three.

Moderately ♩ = 108

P E G G Y   S U E

by Jerry Allison, Norman Petty & Buddy Holly

This pop song was a big hit for Buddy Holly. You will need to count carefully
in bars five and seven to get the rhythm right in the left hand. In fact it would be
a good idea to practise clapping the left hand part in bar five.

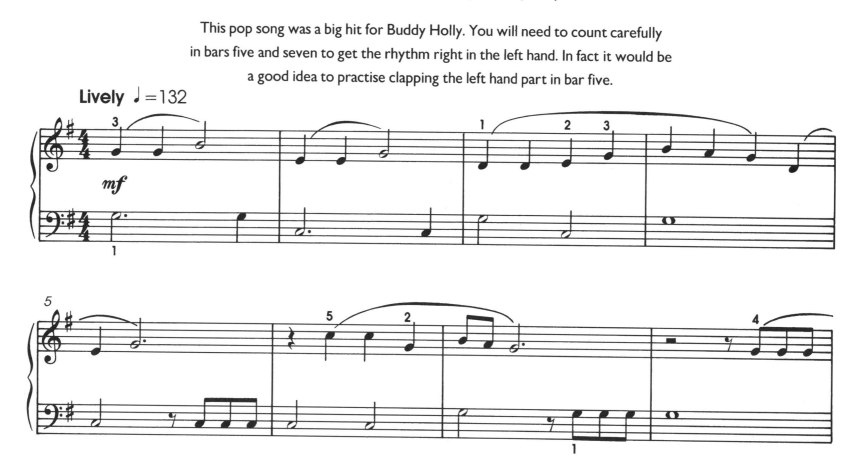

ALL CRIED OUT

by Tony Swain, Steve Jolley & Alison Moyet

Try to make the phrases answer each other.

Make sure there is plenty of difference between the first phrase (loud)

and the second, which is played quite softly (**mp**).

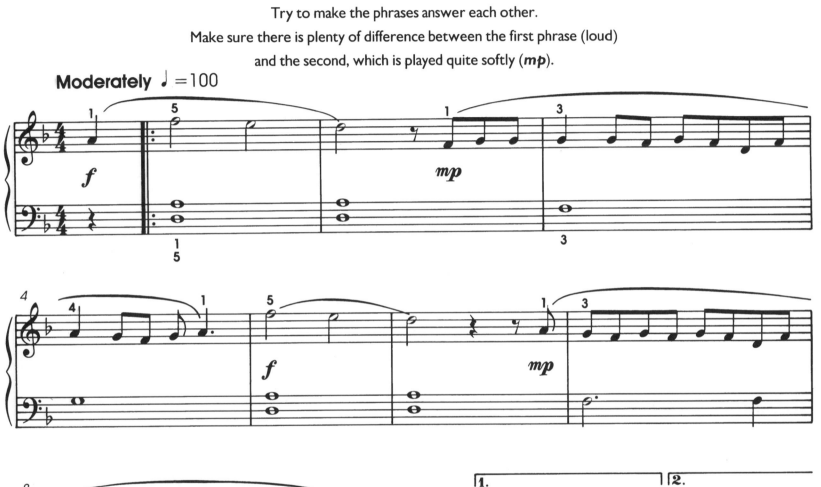

IMAGINE

by John Lennon

In this song John Lennon tried to imagine a world without war.

Take care to observe the rests in the right hand,

and play as smoothly as you can.

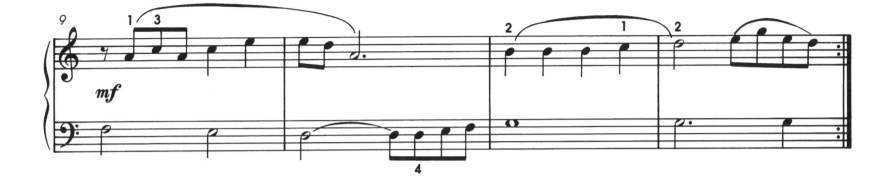

ANNIE'S SONG

by John Denver

Make the right hand tune really sing out above the left hand.
This style of playing is called 'cantabile', which is an Italian word meaning
'in a singing style'. Your playing should be very smooth.

MORNING HAS BROKEN

Traditional

This old hymn tune is still very popular today.

Be careful to let the music 'breathe' between phrases.

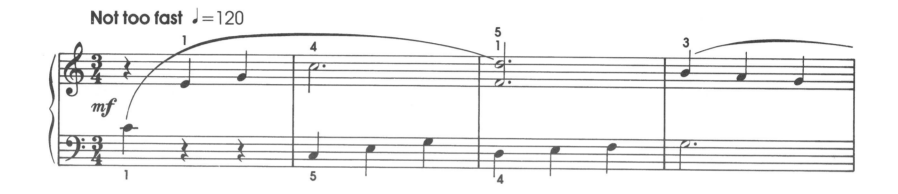

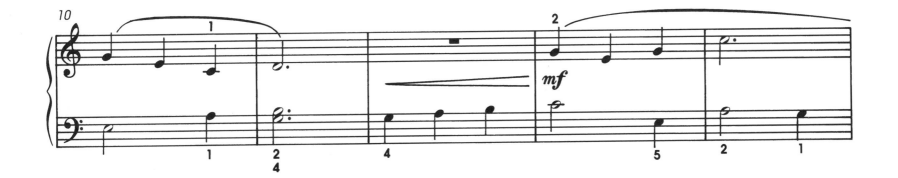

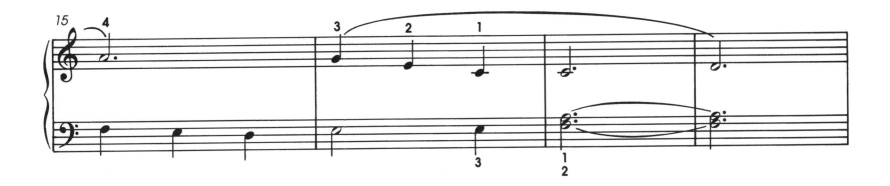

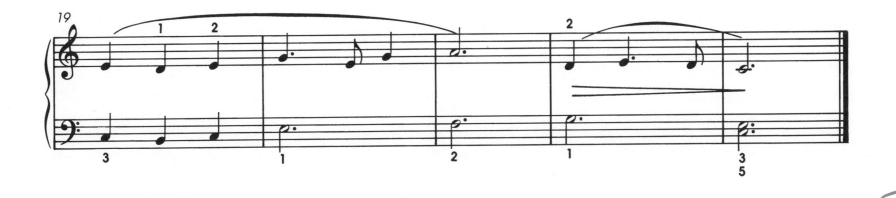

SCARBOROUGH FAIR

Traditional

The main tune of this well-known folk song is in the right hand,
but in bars 9-12 and 21-24 notice how the left hand imitates (copies) the right hand.

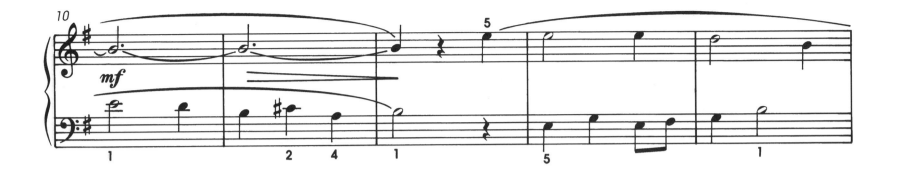

poco rit.

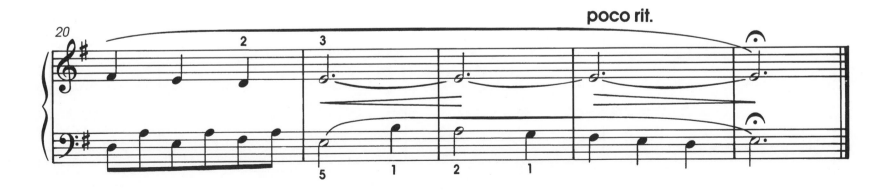

SOMETHING'S GOTTEN HOLD OF MY HEART

by Roger Cook & Roger Greenaway

Try to make the left hand as legato (smooth) as possible.
Practise it separately, making sure that both notes
in the chords sound exactly together.

Moderately ♩=100

THE FIFTY-NINTH STREET BRIDGE SONG

by Paul Simon

Look at the left hand part carefully. Notice how
the first two bars keep repeating all the way through the song.
Practise until you can play them perfectly.

EASTENDERS

by Leslie Osborne & Simon May

This is the theme from the popular television series. Play it at a steady pace,
being careful not to rush the quavers. In bar four alternative fingerings
are given in brackets. Which do you prefer?

Moderately ♩ = 100

HL00363277

U.S. $9.99

8 40126 95535 4

JOHN THOMPSON'S
EASIEST PIANO COURSE

FIRST SMASH HITS

15 pop songs that students will love to play and sing!

WILLIS MUSIC

HAL•LEONARD®

EXCLUSIVELY DISTRIBUTED BY

ISBN 978-1-70513-176-3

9 781705 131763

All Is Found | **from Frozen 2**

Count on Me | **Bruno Mars**

Dynamite | **Taio Cruz**

Firework | **Katy Perry**

Get Back Up Again | **from Trolls**

Havana | **Camila Cabello**

A Million Dreams | **from The Greatest Showman**

Ocean Eyes | **Billie Eilish**

Old Town Road | **Lil Nas X**

Perfect | **Ed Sheeran**

Shallow | **from A Star Is Born**

Shotgun | **George Ezra**

Sign of the Times | **Harry Styles**

Someone You Loved | **Lewis Capaldi**

A Thousand Years | **Christina Perri**

CALIFORNIA DREAMIN'

by John Phillips

Watch out for the first time bars. There are three of them.

Remember to miss them out and go on to the second time bar

when you play the repeat.

EL CONDOR PASA

by J. Milchberg & D. Robles

This old South American tune was made popular by Simon and Garfunkel. Try to make a real contrast in the dynamics, which go all the way from **f** (*loud*) down to **pp** (*very soft*).

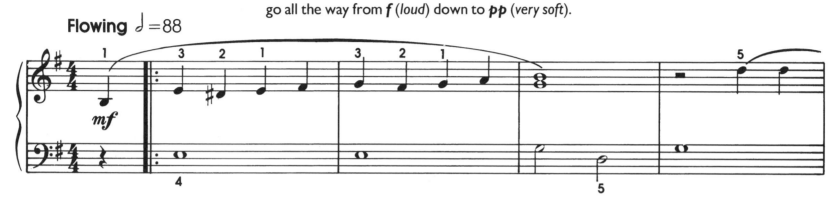

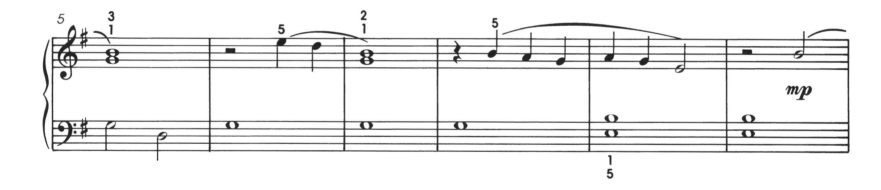

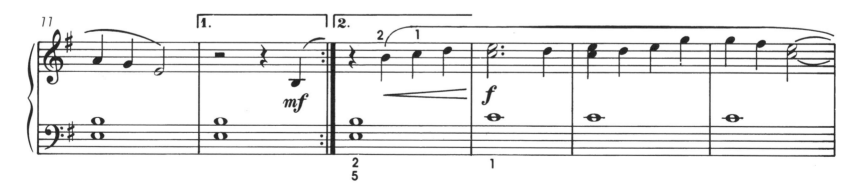

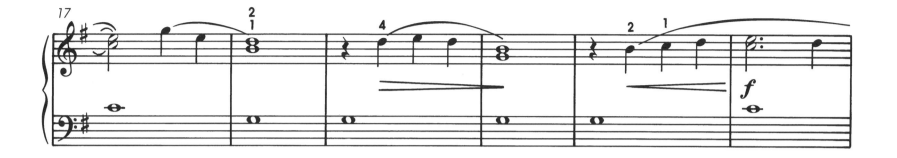

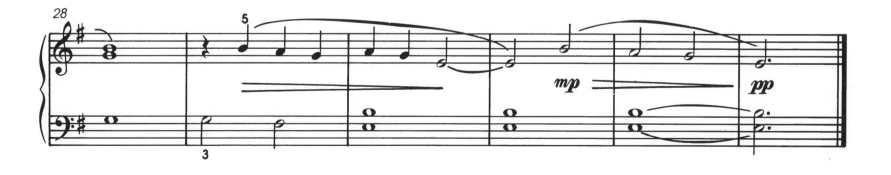

DO-RE-MI

by Richard Rodgers

This song appears in the musical 'The Sound Of Music'.
It was used to teach the children how to sing together. Notice how the
right hand in bars 5-8 is the same as bars 1-4, but a third (three notes) higher.

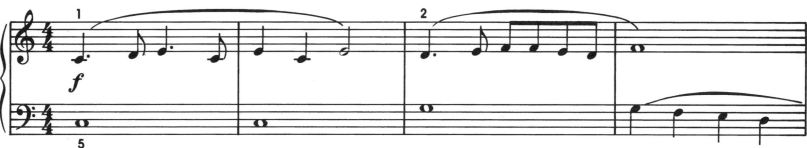

22

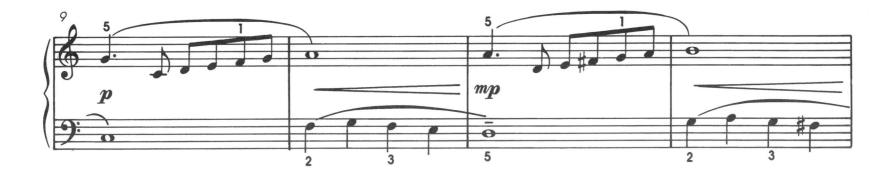

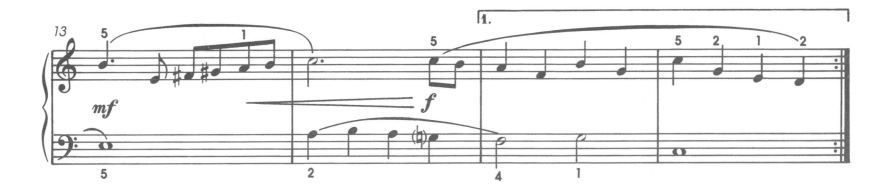

ONE MORE NIGHT

by Phil Collins

The first four bars of this piece are an introduction.

The tune does not begin until bar five, after the double bar-line.

Make sure you count carefully right through.

Expressively ♩=120

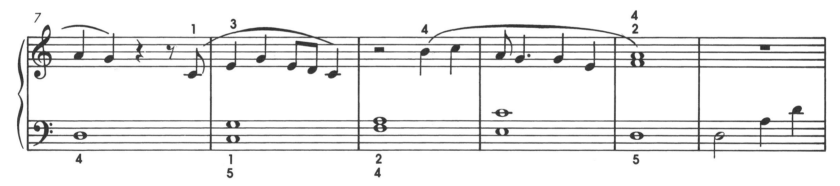

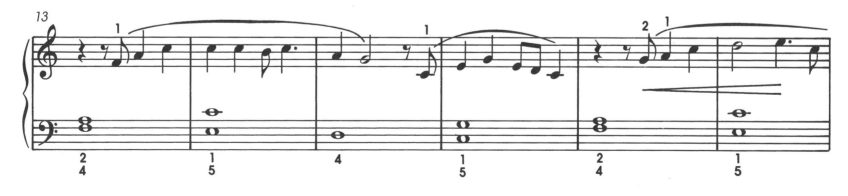

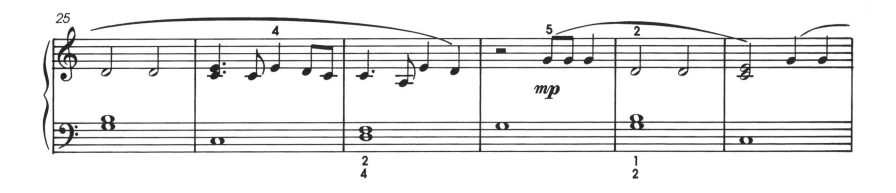

LAST OF THE SUMMER WINE

by Ronnie Hazlehurst

This is the theme from the very popular BBC television series.

Notice that the second half of the piece is almost exactly the same as the first,

but it should be played more quietly.

WE WISH YOU A MERRY CHRISTMAS

Traditional

The left hand has a very interesting part to play in this Christmas Carol.

It is a good idea to practise hands separately before you try to play hands together.

Joyfully ♩=116

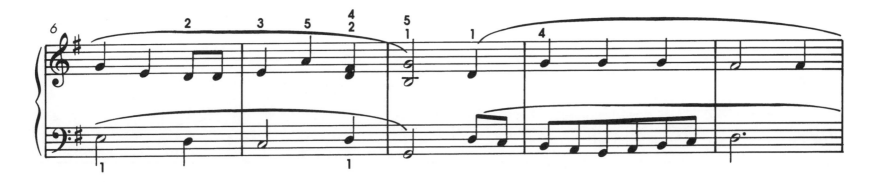

SAILING

by Gavin Sutherland

Both hands play the tune in octaves in the first four bars.
From bar nine the left hand is busy playing quavers. Be sure to keep them
quiet and even, so that the tune in the right hand is clearly heard.

Not fast ♩=80

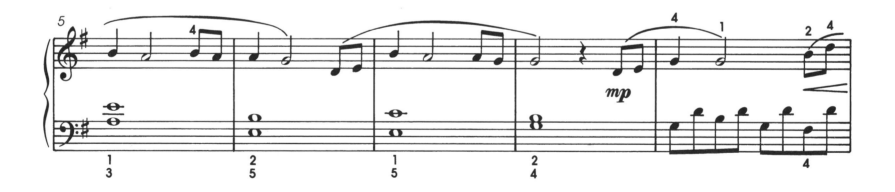

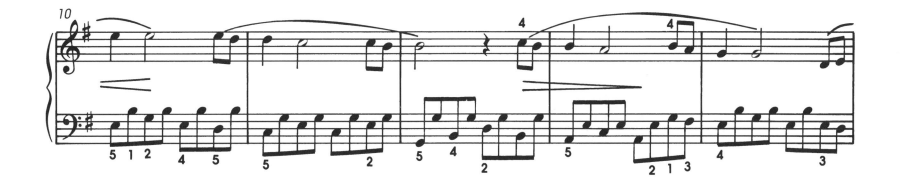

GREENSLEEVES

Traditional

This is a very famous old English tune. It would probably have been sung

by a minstrel, accompanying himself on a lute (a sort of guitar).

Notice that Middle C is sometimes sharp and sometimes natural.

Plaintively ♩ =120

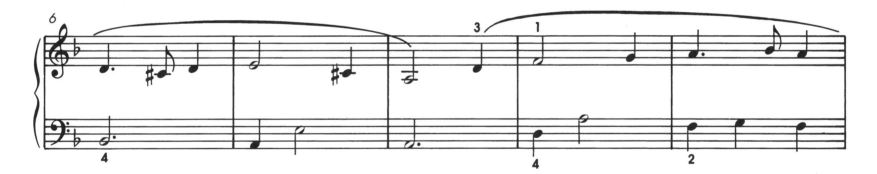

30

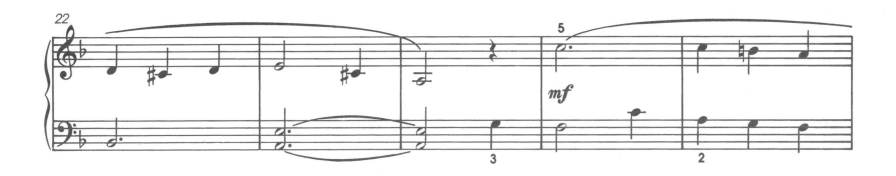

THE SOUND OF SILENCE

by Paul Simon

In spite of the title, don't play this piece too quietly!
Make sure the quavers in the right hand are really even.

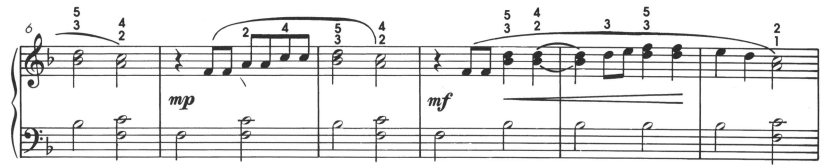

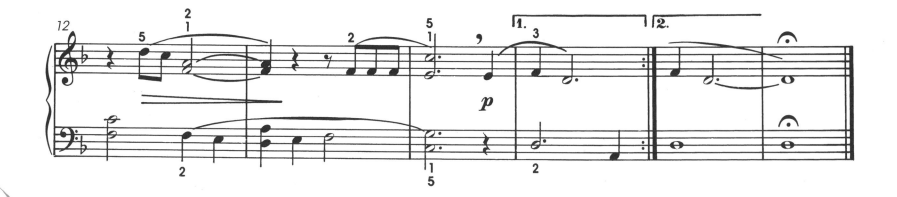